HELLO,

MONDAY!

Courage That Conquers Mountains

TERESA M. COOPER

ISBN 978-1-0980-3180-0 (paperback)
ISBN 978-1-0980-3181-7 (digital)

Christian Faith Publishing, Inc.
832 Park Avenue
Meadville, PA 16335
www.christianfaithpublishing.com

Printed in the United States of America

To my daughter, who is fierce, vibrant, and full of wonder. Crystal Deann Cooper-Taylor, you, my dear, give me great joy.

CONTENTS

FOREWORD

Pastor Teresa has taken some of the most pressing issues of everyday living and given insight into how to conquer through the knowledge of the Word of God. Simple, provocative, enlightening, and relevant.

Monday represents more than a day of the week. It's the day designated to start the process again. It is the day that expects things left undone to be completed. It is the time of addition, adding what was not completed to what must be done. It is the time of reckoning! A day of getting started. It can be a time of dreadful anticipation of the challenges, responsibilities, and endeavors that must be handled successfully.

My impression of Monday is the day after the day of rest (Sunday). As a child growing up in the South, it was the day you returned to the cotton fields, picking cotton under a merciless sun. It was the day of washing clothes by hand, without the benefit of a washing machine. It is the first day of the week of work.

Pastor Teresa captured the essence of what this day represents. She has skillfully turned a day of dread and potential despair to a time of hope. Those who are deep thinkers will find this day to be a mountain, but because of her faith in the Word of God, it has now become a molehill.

Glance through this book and feel the love and optimism flow from it. Keep it by your bedside, and maybe, just maybe, it will help you greet your Monday with anticipation, hope, and respect.

Juanita Crump
Senior Pastor
Five Fold Ministry Christian Center Inc.

ACKNOWLEDGEMENTS

I want to start by giving thanks to the Almighty God for the heart and vision to write a book that honestly reflects the struggle of breaking through barriers and achieving a relentless faith to continue daily on the journey.

Secondly, I would like to acknowledge my life companion Shaun Cooper Sr. Thank you for consistently encouraging and speaking words of wisdom, affirmation, and love. Your friendship has been my greatest treasure.

New Creation Family Church, I love you and I am still humbled by the privilege we have to serve as your pastors. Women of Stature, you keep me seeking for new ways to relate God's magnificent love for you and toward you! I love that we have grown together in our desire to learn and live as Proverbs 31 women.

I also want to recognize the men and women who were unaware of their inspiration in my life through written word, spoken word, or just by being authentically themselves—Katherine Young, Joel Filkey, Sophia Gatlin, Lysa TerKeurst, Lillie McKinney, and Brenda Ashley.

The finish in any effort comes with the participation of many hands that become one to accomplish the task. Thank you, Lula Davidson, Kierston Bartney, Aunshelle White, and Marcus Batson, for keeping the finish line clear.

Lastly, I would like to share my deepest gratitude to Jordana P. Filkey, who has not only been my pastor but a dear friend and mentor, always providing a safe place to land and godly words to launch.

PRELUDE

TREASURE ALONG THE JOURNEY

I decided that I would write this second book on the one subject I am most challenged with presently. The one thing I know for sure because I face it straight on every week and every month. The challenge that has been consistent 52 days a year out of the 365 days for me is My Monday. I call it My Monday because it seems so personal to me each and every time it appears.

I love life. I love the privilege I get to experience life on a daily basis. Yet I never expected to have a love-hate relationship with a day of the week. So as I have navigated through my relationship with

Monday, I have discovered a few gems that have helped me along the way.

These gems are multifaceted. Some are large nuggets and others are small—a variety of precious treasures I will share to help you along your journey and toward your path of resolve and serenity with whatever appears to be insurmountable.

My objective with this book is to help you reach a place where you can confidently exclaim, "Hello, Monday! I greet you with my fierce presence. Let's go!"

WHAT DAY IS IT?

Hello, Monday!

When did I start noticing the significance of a day of the week? When did Monday become so different than Thursday or any other day? The answer to that question still eludes me. I have just come to the realization that the moment I couldn't bless the Lord for a Monday was the day Monday became different than all the other days.

> *"I will praise the Lord at all times. I will constantly speak his praises. I will boast only in the Lord; let all who are helpless take heart" (Psalms 34:1–2, NLT).*

Whenever we allow a day, a task, a life issue to steal our praise of thanksgiving and gratitude, we create a stronghold for negativity, anxiety, and fear to exist in all its boldness. I can remember back when we were first starting out in pioneering our first church. We weren't taking over a previous established church or coming in as an interim pastor at a ministry. We were pioneering! Makes your mind float to Laura Ingalls Wilder's Little House on the Prairie novels. A family forging a new life in uncharted territory. Pioneering involves starting from scratch and creating a vision that people would follow based on the direction God revealed to you in prayer and fasting.

During those early days, we didn't have an established building with traditional office hours or a place where people could come if they needed prayer or spiritual guidance. I remember thinking how wonderful it would be to have a permanent and secure place to meet the needs of God's people on a daily basis. That would be a real blessing and an indicator that we were headed in the right direction in building a viable church community.

Several years later and many different locations down the road, we were blessed with our God property where we started having "normal" business hours to minister as a functional, viable ministry within our community. The self-expectations along with people's expectations caused a slow-creeping dread of Monday mornings. Isn't it ironic the thing we believe would be a blessing somehow turns out to be the very thing we start to despise? The idea or prayer started with all good intentions and sincerity of heart and spirit. The answered prayer comes with the request and the responsibility of the request wrapped within the petition. The rigorous pace of caring for people while creating systems that meet the request of a spiritually hungry congregation, as well as a surrounding community that is hurting, can blur the line of necessity. True religion according to James 1:27 says, *"Pure and genuine religion in the sight of God the Father means caring for orphans and widows in their distress and refusing to let the world corrupt you."*

The moment I took my focus off of true Christ living, helping and reaching the hurting, I subconsciously placed importance on having office time and space to reach people which equated to performance. God isn't in performance He is in relationship. Had I allowed the world's concepts to corrupt me? We can be so unaware of the crippling effects of what society and ministry label as best practice for success.

Expectation can be a tricky balance in life when we have to weigh God's expectation and our self-expectation. The scripture says, *"Come to me, all of you who are weary and carry heavy burdens, and I will give you rest. Take my yoke upon you. Let me teach you, because I am humble and gentle at heart, and you will find rest for your souls. For my yoke is easy to bear, and the burden I give is light"* (Mathew 11:28–30, NLT). The yokes that God is handing out are easier to bear if we allow Him to teach us. Considering God's expectations raises the value of whatever you are investing time, energy, and life into. A self-expectation that is misplaced can quickly become a heavy burden too large for your shoulders to bear. Monday had become that burden for me. What is your Monday? Your heavy burden or expectations you are trying to carry?

Once I realized that I had created this world, not God and this huge Monday of expectations, I could honestly name it and own it. Friend, isn't that the big elephant in the room, owning your realistic or unrealistic expectations within your life? The ability to own the world you have shaped with your words, beliefs, disbeliefs, gratitude, or complaints forces the powers that are trying to hold you hostage to your fate into the marvelous light of truth. John 8:32 says, *"You shall know the truth and the truth shall make you free."* Freedom to denounce all burdens that aren't yours to shoulder and to roll those burdens onto the one who is able to accomplish more with one touch or one encounter than you would have ever been able to do. John 8:36 says, *"So if the Son sets you free, you will be free indeed."* Redirect your expectations on the almighty, all-powerful God, who has an unconditional love for His creation.

His unfailing love was going to enable me to roll My Monday over to Him, for He was the one who had appointed and sent me. I was the creator of My Monday; He was the creator of Monday!

Notes

What is your Monday?

_____
_____
_____
_____
_____
_____
_____
_____
_____
_____
_____
_____
_____
_____
_____
_____
_____
_____
_____
_____
_____

LEVELING THE PLAYING FIELD

Life is a magical gift we all get to experience, whether long or short; we realize it's a gift given by our creator to cherish and honor Him within our timespan.

> *"From His abundance we have all received one gracious blessing after another. For the law was given through Moses, but God's unfailing love and faithfulness came through Jesus Christ" (John 1:16–17, NLT).*

Monday's were coming 52 days a year, without my appreciation or validation, so I was going to need a God strategy to not just encounter Monday but to joyously experience the grace God would provide within my Monday. How could those 52 days feel as if they largely consumed the 365 days that are in one year? Once I was able to identify that Monday had become a spiritual stronghold on my entire week, that's when I discovered the desire to level the playing field. I had created this monster of a day over time, but with a spirit of truth in operation I could quickly ask the Holy Spirit to level Monday with every day of the week and cause me to release all the built up expectations and responsibilities I had so faithfully placed on this day and myself.

Have you ever placed a greater importance on something and that placement caused all other areas in your life to suffer? I had evaluated Monday so high that if one thing went wrong or ran behind schedule, it had the potential to distract the next few days of the week. You might be thinking this is way too analytical and why anyone would actually do this to themselves. Right, who would process their days in such a way? I can only answer from my personal struggle, a person with a high demand and a small staff to accomplish a variety of programs and administrative duties. A person who expects excellence, efficiency, and structure within the work environment and personal life.

As I allowed the Holy Spirit to interrupt my process of doing and thinking, a supernatural grace was released toward me to cast my Monday's cares, expectations, goals onto the Father's shoulders. He is the greatest example of excellence, efficiency, and structure. He created the world in all its grandeur in six days and rested on the seventh. I could learn enormously from that model! I learned to approach my Monday with a rest mentality. Rest, press into your week with a relaxed and well-rested mind that suggests God truly cares. I know my Father sees me and He will give me grace, a favor to accomplish all that concerns me, and what I don't accomplish He will provide another opportunity without lack. He can level the playing field to my advantage without fear of what the day brings. Anxiety is the relative of fear, but the scriptures say, perfect love casts out fear. Oftentimes we applaud ourselves for not being fearful, yet we operate in levels of anxiety that are closely linked to fear.

I work in the nonprofit sector as an administrative pastor for one organization and executive director of another organization. Both of these roles require a great deal of management skills in the office along with time management. If I am not careful to lean on to my restfulness, anxiety can slowly begin to build. The finished product of anxiety manifests as fear—fear that a task will be left undone, fear that deadlines and budgets won't be met. When fear sets in, it brings torment, and torment isn't a kind companion. Before you realize it, you're barricaded in your office, not answering phone calls, and skipping lunch. I'm reminded of a statement my dear pastor Jordana Filkey said to me, "You only toil outside the will and provision of God, Teresa. You're in His will, and He has provided provision. You just need to slow your cadence to mirror His Word. God is for the vision! That's what provision means in its simplicity."

What has you slowly embracing the companion of anxiety and learning more about fear and toil? Could it be owning a business, parenting teenagers, pastoring, being a single parent, or school? All are challenging and worthy missions in life that require guidance on a daily basis from our Heavenly Father. His instructions, according to Mathew 6:26–27, says, *"Look at the birds. They don't plant or harvest or store food in barns, for your Heavenly Father feeds them. And aren't you far more valuable to him than they are? Can all your worries add a single moment to your life?"* Consider your worth to the Father the next time you allow worry or anxiety to carry you away into the abyss of fear, the unknown. Fear and faith are both based on the premise of the unseen. Fear is attached to the unseen negative that could happen. Faith is attached to the unseen positive that could. Fear grows into torment, but when faith grows, it grows in hope. Hope with an expectation! The key is knowing which to feel to obtain the expected outcome on a daily basis.

> *"Don't be impressed with your own wisdom. Instead, fear the Lord and turn away from evil. Then you will have healing for your body and strength for your bones" (Proverbs 3:7–8, NLT).*

Hello, Monday! You are starting to look different.

Notes

What can you level and make an open road?

_____
_____
_____
_____
_____
_____
_____
_____
_____
_____
_____
_____
_____
_____
_____
_____
_____
_____
_____
_____
_____

MOVING THINGS AROUND

I read a quote once that said, "If Monday was a person, I would punch it in the face!" LOL! Truth is a powerful thing! Truth of your present surroundings and your present condition can be the difference between life and death. Seeking for the truth in your life daily can and will produce lasting stability. Again I quote, *"You shall know the truth and the truth shall make you free."* The value of truth is found in the freedom that it brings—freedom to become who God has preordained you to be on earth and in your life, producing the best original version of yourself for the glory of God.

As I began to zero in on how I had made Monday into this insurmountable giant in my life, the power that comes with a realized truth flooded me with the desire to break and conquer that which was trying to control and conquer my days, weeks, and months as they progressed. Truth can come instantly. Sometimes it can be revealed, or it can be unveiled after deep soul searching and reflection. It took me years before I realized the emotional pattern I had created for myself. I had convinced myself that most of the displeasure I was confronted with came with the job description, the demands at home, etc. When I realized I had built a Monday mile-high mountain and I had to climb it each week, I was initially devastated at the world I had created. Secondly, I was ashamed that I allowed this to happen and that I allowed it to skew my vision of my work environment and steal valuable time and years. The demands were real, the deadlines were real, the necessity to multitask was a must, but all these abilities were mine to manage, and I had failed. I had failed at accomplishing these skills with the gracious joy of the Lord that renews and restores our minds when we do all things as unto Him. Failure isn't bad if we allow it to lead us to the corrected path we should've been on all along.

"Work willingly at whatever
you do, as though you were working
for the Lord rather than for people.
Remember that the Lord will give

*you an inheritance as your reward,
and that the Master you are serving is
Christ" (Colossians 3:23–24, NLT).*

When truth was embraced, a freedom came—a freedom to see my humanity, the freedom to ask for eyes of faith to not just climb this mountain but to remove it all together if that be His will.

"Jesus replied, "Have faith in God constantly. I assure you and most solemnly say to you, whoever says to this mountain, 'Be lifted up and thrown into the sea!' and does not doubt in his heart [in God's unlimited power], but believes that what he says is going to take place, it will be done for him [in accordance with God's will]. For this reason I am telling you, whatever things you ask for in prayer [in accordance with God's will], believe [with confident trust] that you have received them, and they will be given to you" (Mark 11:22–24, AMP).

So I began the journey of moving My Monday Mountain by moving things around. Moving the office landscape around and readjusting the atmosphere appeared simple, but it created a new energy and life in my space that I needed. I had been so focused on the Monday climb that I had never considered an atmosphere change. Sometimes you can't change your circumstances immediately; however, you can change how you respond to your circumstances and even add beauty and serenity to your atmosphere. When you reset the mood and add ambience to your surroundings, you elevate your faith and expectations. My husband has a principle that states, "You must release your faith before you arrive." I had to shift my atmosphere by moving things around so my faith could believe beyond what I saw, felt, or touched.

I had to believe My Monday Mountain was removed before it actually materialized. Rearranging my office made it appear new, fresh, and enjoyable again. Adding meaningful color and pictures created a more welcoming presence as well. The simple act of rearranging items in the natural sent ripples in the spirit that faith for change was present. When you believe in something better or more, your spirit tells you to make room for what you believe in. You begin to clean out and give away items to make room for the new.

What needs rearranging in your life? How can you move things around to create another perspective, another view?

> *"But whenever someone turns to the Lord, the veil is taken away. For the Lord is the Spirit, and wherever the Spirit of the Lord is, there is freedom. So all of us who have had that veil removed can see and reflect the glory of the Lord. And the Lord—who is the Spirit— makes us more and more like him as we are changed into his glorious image" (2 Corinthians 3:16–18, NLT).*

Let's start with decluttering our lifestyle and living space to reflect our newfound expectation! "Clutter is the subtle death of success," as my husband, Shaun, would say. The first step to a clearer more expansive view of conquering My Monday Mountain was banishing all forms of clutter. A clutter-free desk, a clutter-free car, a clutter-free briefcase, and all other areas I could declutter became a primary pursuit. You may ask, why? The less complicated and more streamlined my surroundings became, the more I mirrored that reflection. Before long the Monday mountain began to look like a hill, and soon the hill became flat and leveled into an open road. I am thankful for open roads that have turns and forks along the journey of life. It is in those turns and forks in the road we discover a clearer image of ourselves. Trusting in this new clutter-free view was going to be adventurous.

> *"Trust in the LORD with all your heart and do not lean on your own understanding. In all your ways acknowledge Him, And He will make your paths straight"* *(Proverbs 3:5–6, NASB).*

Notes

What things do you need to rearrange?

_____

_____

_____

_____

_____

_____

_____

_____

_____

_____

_____

_____

_____

_____

_____

_____

_____

_____

_____

_____

KNOW YOUR RHYTHM

*"Look straight ahead, and fix
your eyes on what lies before you.
Mark out a straight path for your
feet; stay on the safe path. Don't
get sidetracked; keep your feet from
following evil" (Proverbs 4:25–27,
NLT).*

The phrase *slower is faster* has proven wise and relevant when the open road in front of you is uncharted territory and you're in need of a physical tune-up. The realization that Monday's mountain had been leveled and Monday's hill had been crossed brought extreme levels of release and a joy of contentment. However, how do I now navigate this new open space set before me? The word God spoke to me was, "Teresa, know your rhythm, the pace I have set for you, and navigate your steps to the rhythm and movement of the

Holy Spirit in your life." Immediately, slower became faster! I realized that the rhythm of my life wasn't the same as my spouse's and surroundings. I realized my rhythm had changed with my age, and it changed with the stage of my life as well. All these adjustments or lack of adjustments on my part was causing unnecessary frustration which caused my steps to falter.

Slower is faster doesn't connote procrastination or the lack of passion. The principle I received from this phrase was that focused and measured steps accomplish far more lasting results than quick, swift, short steps with the finish line in view. The finish line or destination zone can at times alter our perception of life. If we don't arrive quickly at our desired destination, we may automatically assume we are off course and that we are navigating through the wrong map of life. I must admit that I have often in my journey looked over into someone else's lane of life and felt as if God had made a mistake in charting my destiny. As if God makes mistakes! Our emotions, when they are not aligned with the Holy Spirit's rhythm, can cause our thought life to veer off into all sorts of falsehoods. When we are in rhythm, we speak out into the atmosphere.

"The steps of a [good and righteous] man are directed and established by the Lord, and He delights in his way [and blesses his path]" (Psalms 37:23, AMP).

My steps are ordered! God knows the way that I take, He is the author of my steps when I walk upright. As Job 23 says,

"But He knows the way that I take [He has concern for it, appreciates, and pays attention to it]. When He has tried me, I shall come forth as refined gold [pure and luminous]" (Job 23:10, AMP).

The revelation that He has concern, appreciates, and pays attention to our steps can instantly suck the life out of every lie in the deception the enemy tries to plant and establish in our thinking.

The goal was to keep me from realizing that God sees me! Out of all the creation, His love zooms in and sees my steps, and He cares. God was pushing me into a necessary continual space of walking in faith in every moment of my day. What I had to resolve in my inner thoughts was that faith is something we never graduate from; it's something we grow in. After twenty-five-plus years of walking with Jesus, my faith was still being stretched and challenged in ways that it hadn't been and in old familiar ways that hadn't surfaced in a while. The scripture says in Habakkuk 2:4, "*Look at the proud! They trust in themselves, and their lives are crooked. But the righteous will live by their faithfulness to God.*" Faith in God and faithfulness to God was how I had lived and how we built our family. Walking in faith wasn't just what we did; it was who we were as followers of Christ. A rhythmic dance of faith!

I can remember as a young married couple being faced with many obstacles and challenges early in our marriage concerning our faith walk and faithfulness to God. We were always given these choices early on. What were we going to build our fundamental principles upon? What would be our core? What would we value and prioritize? One of the first opportunities we had to answer and define those questions was during a time when all our young couples friends were launching into homeownership. I can remember the joy of attending celebrations and housewarming gatherings for all the first-time home buyers. The smell of new construction and designer decorations, and well-organized parties seemed to never end. Finally, I asked Shaun, "When do you think we will be launching into the home buyers frenzy?" We can afford it; we have great credit. I can still remember as a young bride hearing his response, "Well, baby, I feel like the Lord would have us use our finances for ministry and not for a down payment on a house." Ministry! Can you be a little more specific, because all my girlfriends are getting new houses? Specifics, isn't that what we all want? Even if we don't necessarily agree with them, we like specific direction. So ministry came in the form of two brand-new professional saxophones. The beginning of our musical ministry and faithfulness to God was established in that choice between natural desire and ministry calling. The priority was settled in our agreement! Today the music that has been birthed from our decision has literally traveled across the globe touching thousands.

The bible is full of rich and vibrant characters that display an assortment of personality and divine purpose. Of all the characters and bible relationships, I have always felt a deep connection with the story of Martha and Mary, two sisters within a family who had very distinct positions and personalities that were on display as Jesus became acquainted with their family. I have an intimate connection with each of these ladies. I have at times felt as if I had a dueling Martha and Mary living within my spirit. Accepting my rhythm brought a clear acknowledgement that I was a Martha, a worker bee. However, I am also Mary, a worshipper who lives in the moment, eccentric at times. These are both wonderful qualities, and most people operate in one or the other's personality. I discovered that I often vacillate between the two with my Martha characteristics needing boundaries so as to not become too overpowering and my Mary characteristics sitting and worshipping at the feet of my King. Knowing your rhythm brings you into a deeper depth of understanding your character traits.

Years ago in one of my work settings we took a personality test. This particular test we took described our personality using animal characteristics. I thought it was very interesting because I was identified as a lion/beaver personality. Based on the questions you answered and the total number totals, you would have a dominant personality or an even balance of two personality characteristics. I have taken this evaluation survey several times over the years with this same style of survey or with a different type of survey. Each time the results were the same, a strong leader who takes charge, who has a hard-work ethic, is willing to get the small tedious jobs done, and is not afraid to step up with an intimidating attitude. A lion who roars—that's me. A beaver as well who will burn the midnight oil if need be. The me that most people don't see is the Mary that wants to sit at the master's feet and worship and not have concerns as to what needs to be done. Well, I unfortunately haven't discovered that revelation in its entirety. What I have discovered is that when my footsteps are in sync with my course in life, I can faithfully work and worship with my life. Being a doer, a worker bee, is my worship, my portion in the journey.

When we revisit the story, Martha and Mary invited Jesus to their home. The custom of hospitality was the host prepared for the guest and entertained the guest. The real dilemma for Martha was that Jesus wasn't any guest; He was the guest of their lifetime. The responsibility that Martha was carrying was properly hers to handle, as it was her home, and she invited the guest. The real anxiety arose when she noticed that, unlike herself, her sister, Mary, had recognized this was a once-in-a-lifetime guest in a once-in-a-lifetime moment, and she seized it and chose what was best, sitting at His feet so as to not miss a thing! Jesus, as He does, noticed and asked Martha, what was wrong? I have found that same question posed to me: what's wrong, Teresa? Usually the answer is found when I take stock of how I have misappropriated the balance between work and worship. When I haven't listened to the voice of the Holy Spirit saying, "Seize this moment. Rest in this moment. Sit at the Master's feet and learn of Him in this moment." You can be ambidextrous in life; you just need to know when to seize the important moments.

> *"We can make our plans,*
> *but the Lord determines our steps"*
> *(Proverbs 16:9, NLT).*

Notes

Have you discovered your rhythm?

_____
_____
_____
_____
_____
_____
_____
_____
_____
_____
_____
_____
_____
_____
_____
_____
_____
_____
_____
_____
_____

I WAS MADE FOR THIS

> *"Now we see things imper-*
> *fectly, like puzzling reflections*
> *in a mirror, but then we will see*
> *everything with perfect clarity.*
> *All that I know now is partial*
> *and incomplete, but then I will*
> *know everything completely, just*
> *as God now knows me completely"*
> *(1 Corinthians 13:12, NLT).*

That's good news! God knows me completely, and nothing is hidden from Him. In spite of His knowledge, He still loved us and chose us in Him before the world was framed, according to Ephesians 1:4. When we walk in the divine knowing that we were made and positioned for the day we live in, we can lean on to God's providential hand of care in our every step. God's love for you is not based on performance or your goodness. That would make His love conditional, and God's love is unconditional and not born of this world, for God is love.

So many times in our day-to-day life, circumstances try to convince us otherwise. I love His thoughts about us that is clearly made known in Ephesians 1. Before he created light (Sun), darkness (Moon) and gave it purpose, God had already chosen you and me. In fact, the world was framed, and all its functions were put into place with purpose because He chose us! We humans are the object of His affections, created in His image and in His likeness. Remember, the scripture says nothing is or was hidden from Him and He still chose us. We were designed to bring God glory on earth—glory manifested through our lives of obedience and surrender, including cracks and frailties.

My friend, God takes the cracks of life, along with its deficiency, and aggrandizes them. The word *aggrandize* means "to increase the power, status, or wealth of a thing." He increases the value and enhances the power of our story by releasing the work of the Holy Spirit in and through us as we yield and press into His presence. When we are on our own and left to our own thoughts and actions, we become self-destructive and counter-intuitive. It's only when we see ourselves through the lens of God's Word do we truly discover the depth and width of God's love toward us and His compassion poured out on our destiny, a destiny that so eagerly guides and redirects for good when we stay near His mouth to hear His intimate conversation about you.

Recently, while I was studying, I found a very interesting Japanese custom. When the Japanese mend broken objects, they aggrandize the damage by filling the cracks with gold. They believe that when some things suffer damage and have history, they become more beautiful; therefore, valuable things are never completely lost! It's a custom that definitely has godly character and thought running all through it. God, in His infinite love for us, provides the gold standard when we have areas in our lives that are cracked, broken, and irreparable to the natural eye. A verse in Romans so clearly brings it all into perspective when it declares that God will work all things together for our good, those who are the called according to His purpose. Talk about history! My friend, you have history with God before the world began!

You and I are too valuable and have too much history to be discarded because of the cracks and chips in our lives. He said in Romans 8:29 that He knew you in advance, and chose you; then He called you and gave you right standing with Himself. God Himself filled your cracks! And then he gave you His glory, the glory that makes you a magnet to the hurting, disenfranchised, and discarded. What can we say to such deliberate, reckless love? I embrace you and allow you to empower me to confront the daily inequities that try to paralyze my progress and stifle my creativity. Boldly declaring,

> *"I was made for this! If God be for me who or what can be against me? The Lord is for me, so I will have no fear" (Psalms 118:6).*

Walking with that declaration requires no fear of changing surroundings or circumstances, and fully trusting in the creative power of your words to shape or shift the atmosphere you are dwelling in. I can remember other occasions where I had to reset my thinking and my attitude toward agreement with God way before the actual manifestation of change.

> *"Don't copy the behavior and customs of this world, but let God transform you into a new person*

by changing the way you think"
(Romans 12:2, NLT).

At this point in your reading you might ask, why am I writing this book in such a transparent way? Why be so vulnerable and honest with my life experiences? My first response is I don't know how to speak truth or relay the experience without being truly vulnerable with my story. I connect best with issues when I feel unrestricted to speak of them in all of the complexities of the true context and struggle. Once I've conquered it and moved on to a clearer and victorious view, I have the advantage of retrospect and time on my side. As I share my story, it's more of a joy and pleasure to help navigate someone else who may have an insurmountable issue they are facing on a daily basis or a similar journey and can benefit from my guidance and encouragement.

One of the earliest nuggets I learned in my Christian walk was how to identify the manner in which the Lord works in my life. What does His footprint and pattern look like in my story? How does He communicate with me? To answer those questions requires deep thought and time to consider past victories, failures, lessons learned, and trials repeated to bring clarity that reveals finality. Knowing God's track record, the patterns He has used when delivering you and the methods that has worked over your life allow you to embrace His process of overcoming. My pattern was if I stayed open, unafraid to confess my faults, I quickly overcame them. I also learned the power of timing and release, being able to know the right time to release the story of victory from a past struggle. The negative forces of life would like to keep your struggles or difficulties as a ransom over your success. When you allow God to give you a time and release valve, you free yourself from any and every ransom that would keep you in hiding. When you tell your story, you and God control the narrative. When you allow the fear and intimidation of others to assume your story, it usually comes out false. This was how He consistently worked with me, by not allowing me to be comfortable with silent shortcomings.

I can remember the year we spent time in Hot Springs, Arkansas, and our children finally convinced us to take them horseback riding. It was a beautiful fall day with all the autumn leaves turning and pine cones lining along the winding trail. Upon our arrival to the ranch, the owner quickly explained the trail and his years of experience. I eagerly asked, was this a straight trail or a trail that would require elevation at any point? He said, "Madame, this is Arkansas country. You are going to see some of the best views you've ever seen!" I think based on that question alone He chose to position me on one of the older horses and conveniently toward the back with my husband behind me. On my first horse ride, I was going to be on a trail that would elevate and give me prestigious views of the Hot Springs landscape. I was more than nervous! The cowboy was leading the way, the young teens and horses swiftly behind, then my husband and me.

The first sound I made after mounting that grayish-white horse was "Stop! Let me off! And I proceeded to yell this for at least twenty-five minutes before the laughter of my spouse drowned me out and the Cowboy was too far ahead to hear me. *They aren't stopping, Teresa. They will not be distracted by your issues, so you need to find a way to make this experience work and produce a more favorable result because tears and yelling isn't working,* I told myself. In that moment I took in the emotions, and I embraced them, welcomed them to run the length and height of my body until it was done. Once that happened, I slowly began to notice the awesome beauty of my surroundings. How had I missed this? Now I needed to make sure I take complete and full notice of God's creation and its magnificent mountain view now that I was past the emotional breaking point. Isn't that what happens when we challenge ourselves and realize that we are capable of achieving and experiencing things beyond our own limitations? We immediately want to rectify everything we might have missed because of the fear and emotions. I was made for this! To experience the thrill of a horse ride in God's beautiful creation with all the joy it would bring once I allowed myself to receive it. And the record showed that once I released the issue or struggle, it soon became a thing of the past no longer having position in my life.

> *"Roll your works upon the Lord [commit and trust them wholly to Him; He will cause your thoughts to become agreeable to His will, and] so shall your plans be established and succeed"* (Proverbs 16:3, AMP).

You, my friend, were made for this day and for this challenge!

Notes

What have you discovered about yourself and your worth?

_____

_____

_____

_____

_____

_____

_____

_____

_____

_____

_____

_____

_____

_____

_____

_____

_____

_____

_____

_____

GETTING STUCK
WHILE IN MOTION

"Manage your emotions and inner dialogue," as my husband would famously say. Isn't that the real issue? It's not the outside enemies, but it's the enemies within that are the hardest to tame and rid from our lives. When progress is outwardly visible and life is progressing at an unprecedented speed, yet if someone were to ask you, how are you doing? You would easily reply, "I feel stuck." Things are moving and life is happening all around me, yet I feel stuck. I feel stuck because I'm not keeping cadence with the life I envisioned. I see things happening in the earth and I sense things happening in the spirit realm. Yet, I haven't aligned the two with the rhythm of my response to each event. Why is my response delayed?

Could it be that my reflexes are more tuned and conditioned to the signs and whistles of earthly happenings than they are to spiritual happenings? Motion, busy, working, accomplishing, activity—all surmise success. The question is, whose success? Who places the value and declares the definition of a thing? I would say that's God's job to define and place meaning and value on a person or thing. And if that's true—and He is never stuck but always in motion, forward in action and expression—then the real issue is that I have been spiritually unplugged.

> *"Yes, I am the vine; you are the branches. Those who remain in me, and I in them, will produce much fruit. For apart from me you can do nothing" (John 15:5, NLT).*

What was I attempting to accomplish? Was there evidence of peace, joy, and a God harvest? Several questions began nagging at my heart until I finally reached the end of my questions and sought much needed counsel to bring clarity. I'm reminded of the moment I reached out to my spiritual father for guidance during that time in my life when I felt stuck in the maze of production and demand with no end in sight. I was crying out, "Does God see me, how hard I'm working and achieving without proper aid and support?" I told him, "I'm a one-woman machine who has mastered multitasking." As I continued to verbally release all of my anxieties and frustrations in our conversation, he patiently waited for me to stop, and then he replied, "Teresa, it's not your performance that captures God's attention. It's your complete dependence on Him."

> *"God blesses those who are poor and realize their need for him, for the Kingdom of Heaven is theirs" (Matthew 5:3, NLT).*

Our affection and need for Father God keeps us in the posture of complete humility mixed with undying pursuit for His presence and guidance in our daily endeavors. It's about dependency! God appreciates my work and effort, but it's my complete devotion of faith and a faith that is solely committed to Him that activates the realm of the supernatural to me and for me. *Supernatural*, "beyond what is natural; unexplainable by natural law."

The experience of the Proverbs 31 woman isn't about being perfect; it's about being useful. The virtue she contained was being able to demonstrate all her abilities to produce a lifetime harvest that yielded dividends for her entire family. A return that yields over time, not based on our urgent need for instant gratification, is what's required to become a consistent person of selflessness.

John 15:4 (NLT) says, *"Remain in me, and I will remain in you. For a branch cannot produce fruit if it is severed from the vine, and you cannot be fruitful unless you remain in me."*

What a wonderful promise! Stay connected and you will always be fruitful and useful. When we attempt to live productive lives based on performance and separate from an intimate connection daily with a Christ's infusion we ultimately become disillusion with whatever it is we were focused on accomplishing. I love how 1 Peter 4:2 says, *"You won't spend the rest of your lives chasing your own desires, but you will be anxious to do the will of God."* Seeking and doing His will on a conscious daily basis makes you more aware of every decision and the fruit it will yield.

As we continue, the scripture in 1 Peter 10–11 says, *"God has given each of you a gift from his great variety of spiritual gifts. Use them well to serve one another. Do you have the gift of speaking? Then speak as though God himself were speaking through you. Do you have the gift of helping others? Do it with all the strength and energy that God supplies. Then everything you do will bring glory to God through Jesus Christ. All glory and power to him forever and ever! Amen.*"These verses beautifully display the actions of the Proverbs 31 woman and every person who strives to walk out their gifts in action on a daily basis. The ability to be generational and have a spirit that reflects the greater good of all those who God has positioned in your life comes by divine supply. When the source of your strength and energy is derived from natural sources rather than the eternal source, you soon become depleted. To be depleted is defined as lacking in power, value, or substance. As a believer in Jesus Christ, we should never become depleted as a state of being. Any encounters we may have with the lack of value or substance can immediately be resolved when we release the greater one who dwells on the inside of us.

> *"Now all glory to God, who is able, through his mighty power at work within us, to accomplish infinitely more than we might ask or think. Glory to him in the church and in Christ Jesus through all generations forever and ever! Amen"* (Ephesians 3:20–21, NLT).

What a wonderful realization that He accomplishes and we surrender to His finished work in our story. As Bishop Mark Filkey would say, *"You frame your world by the words you speak! You possess the creative power of God to shape your world."* This power is inherent to all born-again believers who dare to exercise it. Get unstuck in your mind, and your inner and outer world will begin to move in conjunction with God's present motion.

No more seasons, just the state of being in present hope anchored in faith!

Notes

What do you need to unplug from?

_____
_____
_____
_____
_____
_____
_____
_____
_____
_____
_____
_____
_____
_____
_____
_____
_____
_____
_____
_____

Loving the Steps Not the Destination

> *"And I am certain that God, who began the good work within you, will continue his work until it is finally finished on the day when Christ Jesus returns" (Philippians 1:6, NLT).*

It has been twenty-seven years since my husband and I launched as missionaries from California to establish a multicultural, cross-generational, and interdenominational ministry in Shreveport, Louisiana. Since that time as founding pastors, we have had the privilege to mentor and to prepare hundreds of people for discipleship, fivefold ministry and launch several church plants. I can tell you that in twenty-seven years there's almost nothing we haven't experienced.

I say almost because we are still on this adventurous journey. We have experienced culture shock, religious bias, racism, denominational barriers, class consciousness, economic disparity, and national pride all at levels we were unacquainted with, being from a state like California. To my surprise, most of these experiences were not within the twenty-seven years' time span but rather suddenly during the first five years. Talk about severe traumatic shock to the human spirit! Wow, how were we going to fulfill God's vision we so eagerly said yes to, with two small impressionable children who only knew all the colors of the rainbow as family and friends?

There were all new questions we hadn't considered when we left California on January 2, 1993, with a U-Haul containing all of our belongings, our two children, and a young prodigy. From that moment when we arrived in the state of Louisiana, the atmosphere itself greeted us with all the wonder of "Yes, you are in a new geographical place!" It was in those early years and moments that I began to understand that the task God had entrusted us with was going to be a long walk and not a sprint. Hebrews 12:2 says, *"We do this by keeping our eyes on Jesus, the champion who initiates and perfects our faith."*

The challenges that came with being transplants in a state where we had no friends, known family, or cultural history as Southerners was going to require a new level of faith, both spiritually and naturally, for us to advance at every level in our new surroundings. I soon realized that we were prepared for the spiritual task but severely unprepared for the culture and traditions associated with being Southerners. We came to spread the gospel of Jesus Christ and the good news of having an authentic relationship with Him. We knocked on doors, walked sidewalks, hosted radio programs, and eventually became the first African American couple to host a weekly television broadcast in our city—all in the midst of the largest church buildings we had ever seen and where alcohol wasn't sold on Sunday and retail malls didn't open until after one on Sundays. There were so many obstacles we hardly had time to focus on them because they were so numerous. My husband and I were both ordained ministers, and we both accepted the call. Together we were going to pastor this soon thriving ministry that we would build by faith with the word and vision God had given to us both.

We soon discovered that team ministry was an unacceptable approach or concept in our new geographical location. Friend, isn't it funny how God leaves out all the intricate details as He is calling us to go and do? I've come to learn that if He revealed all the intricate details, we might be tempted to decline because of our fear of the known and unknown details. Our obedience is best revealed when we respond out of our trust in Him and the power of His spoken promise. He told Jeremiah, *"I knew you before I formed you in your mother's womb. Before you were born I set you apart and appointed you as my prophet to the nations" (Jeremiah 1:5, NLT).* "Jeremiah, basically I have marked your destiny! Your path has been made clear." And as we have all done, Jeremiah makes an exception for himself. He reminds the Lord of his age and what he can't do for Him. The response of the Lord is one without question: *"Don't say, I'm too young; for you must go wherever I send you and say whatever I tell you. And don't be afraid of the people, for I will be with you and will protect you. I, the Lord, have spoken" (Jeremiah 1:7, NLT)!*

God gives you His word, according to Psalm 138:2–3, *"For your promises are backed by all the honor of your name. As soon as I pray, you answer me; you encourage me by giving me strength."* That is the strength and the courage you need, and it was what we needed as well to conquer the many obstacles that we were confronted with while establishing our ministry. The goodness of God was demonstrated when we embraced the understanding that the destination wasn't the goal. We all have images in our heart of what our journey should look like. If you're like me, you envision more sunny days than cloudy ones and unending fields of sunflowers and tulips. The arrivals of life will be epic, filled with accolades, awards, and cheers of appreciation for all the hard work and endurance. You will arrive! Destination will be accomplished.

Well, there's nothing like pastoring a congregation of people to strip the covers off of all carnal allusions and selfish desire. Ask Moses. It was one thing to find the courage and obedience to follow God and lead His people out of bondage, but it was something altogether different to lead them into a promise land with a living God. Deliverance can be an immediate action that happens swiftly with fervency. Freedom, on the other hand, offers a new way of thinking, liberty, and unfamiliar concepts that require attention to nurture this newfound way of being. The path taken to lead a people successfully to their Promise Land will be one that focuses on the steps and not the destination. When we make the destination the goal, we can easily become so distracted with getting there that we miss all the important, relevant milestones along the way.

The details become a means to an end and not life and character for sustainability. At each step of the journey Moses was traveling with the children of Israel, they were experiencing monumental moments that were stripping the bondage of Egypt off of the people and bringing them into a greater trust and dependence on God. When we view their journey in the book of Numbers chapter 20, we discover a major detail that Moses makes minor because his focus becomes blurred and his hearing dull to the instructions of the Lord. Could it have been the length of the journey? The grumbling of the people? The personal loss within his family? Or was it a combination of all these things that prompted Moses to break away from God's instructions?

> *"As the people watch, speak to the rock over there, and it will pour out its water. You will provide enough water from the rock to satisfy the whole community and their livestock" (Numbers 20:8, NLT).*

Satisfying the congregation of Israel or finally getting them to stop complaining and blaming him for their suffering, and journeying on to freedom could have been a real human emotion that potentially contributed to Moses response.

> *"'Listen, you rebels!' He shouted. Must we bring you water from this rock? Then Moses raised his hand and struck the rock twice with the staff, and water gushed out. So the entire community and their livestock drank their fill. But the Lord said to Moses and Aaron, 'Because you did not trust me enough to demonstrate my holiness to the people of Israel, you will not lead them into the land I am giving them!'" (Numbers 20:10–12, NLT).*

Like Moses, how many times have we left God's presence after hearing His instructions and chosen to respond from a fleshly realm and not from His guided presence? When we find ourselves responding from a nature that doesn't emulate the directive God has clearly given, we must check our motives. When our motives become attached to self-gratification, ease, pleasure, and our preconceived outcomes, we disconnect from His voice guiding our step as we journey.

I can remember times when we became severely frustrated with the growth pattern of our congregation and the perceived outcome we had expected. It was in those moments the Holy Spirit would gently whisper, *"I have made a wide path for your feet to keep them from slipping"* (Psalms 18:16). Trust the steps and dig in deep and don't lose focus of His word, and it will carry you through the process.

The process is what produces the finish product. In other words, it's the completion of every step along the assembly line that ensures all the components are developed properly. When we, by choice or negligence, choose to alter the process, we create defective outcomes—outcomes that don't reflect God's original blueprint and design. Every time my husband and I as leaders tried to alter God's time, process, or plan, we gave opportunity for a defect in our life and in the lives of those we provided spiritual oversight. It's so important that we allow natural integration and adjustment to have its full process.

It naturally took a full, well-lived decade mixed with patience, understanding, love, acceptance, and respect for our family to receive an authentic Southern welcome. The organic nature of our reciprocal relationship taught us a great deal about influencing people at the point of their reference. It also taught us more about God's compassionate grace and the strength of our faith to model what love is versus what love says. Thank God for grace that covers our frailty and provides correction to keep us on course. I love that God is a finisher in our lives. He declared our success before we started, and He made provision for every one of our mistakes.

In God's big design He allowed Moses to see the Promise Land even though he couldn't lead the children of Israel into the Promise Land. However, because God is the God of the finish, we read in Mathew 17 that Jesus took James, Peter, and John to a high mountain to be alone and something supernatural occurred. *"Suddenly, Moses and Elijah appeared and began talking with Jesus. Peter exclaimed, "Lord, it's wonderful for us to be here! If you want, I'll make three shelters as memorials one for you, one for Moses, and one for Elijah."* Moses accepted the steps and finished his earthly journey, and God, the Alpha and the Omega, brought Moses full circle to stand in the Promise Land with the Messiah, the Redeemer, our Mighty Deliverer! Mountain top views are the most transforming.

Notes

Are you loving the steps?

_____
_____
_____
_____
_____
_____
_____
_____
_____
_____
_____
_____
_____
_____
_____
_____
_____
_____
_____
_____
_____

I Have Permission

It's okay! He really does make all things new.

The joy a young person has when they make their first adult decision, whether it's financial or adventurous, is very exhilarating, especially when they have approval from a parent. The freedom of consent opens doors that may have been hidden. My husband, Shaun, has a principle that says, "Freedom without boundaries is bound for abuse." I'm in love with the liberty that God has revealed and released unto us if we would just believe and receive this enormous liberation of love. Often we spend days and countless hours focused on what we can't do or what restrictions we feel have been placed upon us by society, religion, family, friends, and on and on that we become numb to the awesome freedom Christ has purchased for us. It's a freedom to love, freedom to forgive, freedom to start again because we have permission.

I remember years ago when we were still raising our teenage daughter, my father-in-law said to my husband and I, "Son, if you don't teach her how to trust herself and her heart, how will she ever learn the confidence she is going to need to navigate in the world?" He continued by saying, "You must give her levels of freedom so she can learn her judgment or lack of judgment to gain confidence in what she has been taught." He was simply articulating the principle of permission. Give her parental permission to grow up. Crystal, who is now a wonderful wife, mother, and woman of God, has blossomed in her personality, creativity, and awareness, as we realized our affirmation and permission, intentionally given, released her to soar in ways we didn't know were possible.

God's affirmation is so similar in nature. Once we realize we have it and then we truly receive it, it makes everyone else's approval null and void, unnecessary. I say unnecessary because we will no longer validate ourselves based on other people's approval or disapproval. We begin to qualify and measure our success by God's permission slip. His written word is our permission slip, and He signed it with His blood.

We can and we do because He has given us authorization to be more than a conqueror! When our level of truth in God's Word reaches that depth, the reservoir of possibility becomes endless. What our past history looks like and what our natural qualifications are may become obsolete when they are compared against Father God's permission. His permission for you to excel, to expand, and to reach new heights spiritually, physically, and financially has the ability to send ripple effects into generations born and unborn.

Giving myself permission to accept areas of weakness in my life hasn't always been easy to do. I am by nature a very strong willed person. I have had a strong sense of core stability inwardly as long as I can remember. The early awareness that I wasn't the popular, carefree, outgoing, all-American type of personality but more of the head-in-your-books, odd, blend-in-and-don't-make-waves type of personality made me a predictable, overachieving, dependable American girl. I was dependable; therefore I had responsibilities placed on my shoulders, some by choice and some not by my choosing. When responsibility is placed upon a person early in life, it can at times thrust a person into being exposed to the spirit of perfectionism and unrealistic realities. The moment I discovered the scripture that declares *"in my weakness He is made strong" (2 Corinthians 12:9–*

10), God's approval became alive in me, and I was able to release the overwhelming pressure to be in total control of the outcome and to singularly shape the narrative.

> *"Taste and see that the Lord is good. Oh, the joys of those who take refuge in him" (Psalm 34:8, NLT)!*

My weakness and limitations can find refuge in Him, and with Him I can accomplish all things. *Accomplishing* is a term I am fondly familiar with. Embracing the grace of God over my accomplishments and His methods and patterns over my analytical, dissecting behavior and thinking created a realm of serenity, the quality or state of being still or calm, that I desperately needed—a state of being that I had preapproval purchased by God Himself. "Confront the dark parts of yourself, and work to banish them with illumination and forgiveness. Your willingness to wrestle with your demons will cause your angels to sing. Use the pain as fuel, as a reminder of your strength" (August Wilson).

> *"But He knows the way that I take [He has concern for it, appre-*

> *ciates, and pays attention to it].*
> *When He has tried me, I shall come*
> *forth as refined gold [pure and*
> *luminous]" (Job 23:10, AMP).*

Self-permission is powerful within its own right, but to realize and conceptualize the Creator's consent to be authentically yourself and to be fully awake on your life journey is truly spiritually liberating on every imaginable level. The struggles and shadows of life work to create a daily mirage or fracture in our ability to be centered and unafraid to look at our frailties and human walls of protection we have surrounded ourselves with. Once we pierce through those barriers, we instinctively become aware of our need for the source, God the creator, to reveal Himself and His purpose for our lives. God the Creator, the originator of purpose, provides the solution for every segment of our life that has become misaligned and misappropriated. He knows the function and releases the remedy through His son, Jesus Christ *(Ephesians 1:23)*.

Notes

What do you have permission for?

_____
_____
_____
_____
_____
_____
_____
_____
_____
_____
_____
_____
_____
_____
_____
_____
_____
_____
_____
_____

BELIEVE

*"How happy you are to believe
that the Lord's message to you will
come true" (Luke 1:45, NLT).*

Belief—it's a powerful dynamic necessary for living a life that flourishes and cultivates the environment in which you live. When we take on the idea of loving the steps and not the destination, we enter a realm of pure belief anchored in hope and rooted in faith. To transition your way of thinking from life's arrivals to life's daily steps requires a now faith, faith for the very present knowing that God has already completed your victorious finish.

He is the God of the Destination!

*Faith is the confidence that
what we hope for will actually
happen; it gives us assurance about*

> *things we cannot see. Through*
> *their faith, the people in days of old*
> *earned a good reputation. Hebrews*
> *11:1–2 (NLT)*

One of my great motivators for writing this book, *Hello, Monday!* was the reality that this Monday mountain wasn't going anywhere. It was a fixture in my story. It came with the ambience of my life, an unassailable position at best, and if this fixture wasn't moveable, I must elevate my faith when approaching. Elevate, rise higher than whatever is standing in front of you. How do I articulate the necessity to pierce through an obstacle that will not vanish but rather appear everyday of your natural life? I heard a quote that said, "Don't spend all our energy trying to figure out how to get out of the desert. Learn everything about how to live in the dessert." Switch your strategy; learn everything about what it takes to fight giants, climb mountains, and navigate uncharted terrain. We so often dedicate enormous amount of time, energy, and passion toward things that we can't change. Time can be easily lost, but when redirected accordingly, we discover abilities and information that were within reach but lay dormant due to inactivity and unawareness.

Listen, no one chooses to live in the desert, but if it is in the providential will of God we find ourselves standing in the desert, how we perceive that reality will be the difference between living and surviving in the desert. You win! And when we believe in God's sovereignty and its inimitable nature, we can know that He controls and creates life in the desert and in unfavorable environments.

> *"For the Lord your God is bringing you into a good land—a land with streams and pools of water, with springs flowing in the valleys and hills" (Deuteronomy 8:7, NLT).*

I will never forget the clarity that came to my mind and spirit regarding our new life as transplants in Louisiana. God's will for our family wasn't for us to survive the relocation; it was His will for us to fully live, embrace, and authenticate His vision for our family in Louisiana. What does that look like? Embracing self and all its uniqueness and silencing all the voices that scream and claw at you to just assimilate. "Shrink, become small, and align yourself with your surroundings. Life and comfort will welcome you like an old friend." It sounds really nice, and we were actually in need of real friends, but the easy road wasn't ours to take. Our road was the way of the Spirit, to believe in the divine work of the Spirit over our destiny. That same choice is yours today to believe in expectations that, not only are you sufficient, you have been made more than enough with Christ.

> *"The poor and needy search for water, but there is none; their tongues are parched with thirst. But I the Lord will answer them; I, the God of Israel, will not forsake them. I will make rivers flow on barren heights, and springs within the valleys. I will turn the desert into pools of water, and the parched ground into springs (Isaiah 41:17–18, NKJV).*

As He brought forth fruitfulness from our life, ministry, and relationships, He strengthened our belief that with His infinite love and care, He dresses every exposed area of our lives to bring Him glory. He provides water in the desert.

"This is what the Lord says—
he who made you, who formed you
in the womb, and who will help
you: Do not be afraid, O Jacob, my
servant, Jeshurun, whom I have
chosen. For I will pour water on the
thirsty land, and streams on the dry
ground; I will pour out my Spirit
on your offspring, and my bless-
ing on your descendants. They will
spring up like grass in a meadow,
like poplar trees by flowing streams"
(Isaiah 44:2–4, NIV).

Whatever our challenges might be or how they might appear in our life, we trust that God provides the adequate resources for us to not just live but to even thrive in the presence of our affliction. The greatest teacher at times is our pain coupled with impending fear. We discover hidden pockets void of the love of God, for perfect love casts out fear. Cast out fear! Daily decry your liberation from fear and all its trappings. Believe!

"On the last and greatest day
of the Feast, Jesus stood and said in

a loud voice, 'If anyone is thirsty, let him come to me and drink. Whoever believes in me, as the Scripture has said, streams of living water will flow from within him.' By this he meant the Spirit, whom those who believed in him were later to receive (John 7:37–39a, NIV).

Notes

What do you believe in?

_____

_____

_____

_____

_____

_____

_____

_____

_____

_____

_____

_____

_____

_____

_____

_____

_____

_____

_____

_____

_____

THE AIR IS
CLEAR ON TOP,
THE MOUNTAIN AIR!

> *"I waited patiently for the Lord to help me, and he turned to me and heard my cry. He lifted me out of the pit of despair, He set my feet on solid ground and steadied me as I walked along"* Psalms 40:1–2, NIV).

Air quality isn't something that most people wake up and have on the recess of their thoughts every day. Regardless, the quality of our air is vital to our health and the overall health of our physical body. Air quality could be listed among the silent killers of humanity. As long as it goes unnoticed and undertreated, it can wreak havoc on an unsuspecting victim. Air quality is affected by air pollution coming from a variety of human-made sources. I'm not an environmentalist or an advocate for climate control; however, I am making an observation on a naturally pure substance called air that becomes hostile to its inhabitants because of their treatment. The treatment can become so severe that what was created to provide and sustain life now belabors and potentially stops life.

It's ironic that a state like California that hosts some of the most majestic views of nature and is known for its ocean, lakes, and healthy lifestyle, according to *State of the Air 2016* by the American Lung Association, has cities and counties at the top of the highest risk for pollution year round and short-term. Monterey County has the cleanest air in the United States for a county! The most aesthetically perfect places can neglect the very thing that sustains its worth—air! How often have we taken for granted our atmosphere both naturally and spiritually? Breathe in, breath out is what we do to live without any thought until our breathing is impaired. What foreign substance or concepts have we allowed to enter into our air space? What unauthorized activity as a Christ follower have we become intimate with to the point that it has literally shifted the very atmosphere we live in? Ask the hard questions as you are climbing your way up or out of whatever barrier that has tried to slow your acceleration to the top.

> *"Wherein in time past ye walked according to the course of this world, according to the prince of the power of the air, the spirit that now worketh in the children of disobedience"* (*Ephesians 2:2, NKJV*).

The key word is in times past! We are now children of the light who pull down thoughts and unauthorized spirits that contradict the will and word of the Father over our lives. The unauthorized pollutants of the atmosphere reduce visibility, and that reduced visibility is the sign that they're present. When the smog of life hinders us from seeing our victorious future and the milestones that we have crossed, our visibility has been tampered with due to pollution. Polluted thinking, confession, and polluted people all tamper with the air quality in our life. One of the first indicators that our body begins to show signs of pollution is with our breathing. The lung's capacity to take in and hold oxygen becomes difficult and mobility eventually stops.

Lack of motion and limited visibility are two things the enemy would love to make you buy into as a permanent way of living. No, my friend, we don't accept atmospheres; we shift atmospheres!

> *"That is why we never give up. Though our bodies are dying, our spirits are being renewed every day. For our present troubles are small and won't last very long. Yet they produce for us a glory that vastly outweighs them and will last forever! So we don't look at the troubles we can see now; rather, we fix our gaze on the things that cannot be seen. For the things we see now will soon be gone, but the things we cannot see will last forever"* (2 Corinthians 4:16–18, NLT).

We fix our gaze, and we climb the mountain, seeking to reach the summit to gain the air, albeit thin—the purest of air because it's our godly right to pursue and achieve our best life now and for eternity. Air pollution is known to cause developmental harm, premature deaths, asthma, susceptibility to infection, and cardiovascular issues. We must become our own advocate and personal EPA agency to ensure we barricade our spiritual immune system from man-made illness. I love that even when we may be the cause of our pollution, God promises in Isaiah 30:19–21,

> *"He will be gracious if you ask for help. He will surely respond to the sound of your cries. Though the Lord gave you adversity for food and suffering for drink, he will still be with you to teach you. You will see your teacher with your own eyes. Your own ears will hear him. Right behind you a voice will say, "This is the way you should go," whether to the right or to the left."*

He is committed to your outcome! He uses every failure, adverse circumstance, and limitation to teach you about His immutable love for and toward you. And that love calls and beckons us to heights we never thought were imaginable. He becomes your guide and trainer for the next level of breakthrough in your journey. Quitting isn't an option, but climbing new heights alone isn't an option either. When I began researching how to prepare for climbing, two major components kept coming up in every article or instruction manual I read: (1) mental strength and (2) never climb alone. For parallelism, we recommend using company.

Assessing your mental strength is paramount. A lot of mountain climbing is about your mental attitude because you will need to make sound, fast judgments about conditions, directions, and safety. As a man thinks, so is he; therefore, if you mentally see yourself achieving and ascending higher altitude, then with Christ you will ascend. I can remember a time in my life when I thought I would always struggle with a certain level of regret because I didn't finish my college degree. I chose to put my higher education on hold to travel with my husband across the nation as an evangelist in the late eighties. We homeschooled our son, and off we went as a family of four across the United States. I believed at the time that was my response to the voice of God calling us forward to uncharted roads of faith and dependency on His direction.

I knew God had given me direction to travel and not attend college, but I wasn't quite prepared for the years of unauthorized chatter that had no respect for God's direction or His plan for my life and my obedience. So as we traveled and crossed genres economically, socially, and racially, there was always this questioning of, am I truly prepared? Which equated to adequacy. Am I enough? That fracture in your thinking can weaken your mental strength and make you unfit for climbing. You become dangerous to yourself and to those who are on your team. Being overconfident is not a desirable trait either, as it can lead you into serious trouble when climbing as well.

Being loaded down by nonessential gear is not an option for a mountain climber. So began God's slow stripping down of my thinking to unload all the nonessential ideas and philosophies that didn't mirror His thoughts of me. He lovingly says, *"You are my servant "For I have chosen you and will not throw you away. Don't be afraid, for I am with you. Don't be discouraged, for I am your God. I will strengthen you and help you. I will hold you up with my victorious right hand" (Isaiah 41:9–10).* You were designed for more! And God says, "Together we will unpack all the nonessential baggage that you're carrying so you can accomplish what I have set before you within your life to finish."

The second necessary technique for mountain climbing is to never climb alone. Wow, so climbing mountains isn't a solo sport or task. It isn't quite like boxing or tennis where you are truly competing with your best self and secondarily your opponent. At least that's what my husband tells me. He was the Northern California Golden Glove Champion Lightweight Division back in his younger years and on his way to the Olympics when he gave his heart to Jesus and had a complete career and life goal change!

The most valuable principle in scaling insurmountable mountains in life is to never climb alone. Everything within you will try and push you to the edge of isolation and self-preservation, but you must fight that false narrative. It isn't real! Every great achievement in successful people's lives happened because those people surrounded themselves with a support team, a scout team, and a skilled climb team.

Proverbs 11:14 says, *"Where no counsel is, the people fall: but in the multitude of counsellors there is safety."* Not only will God Himself advise you He will provide people to speak into your next level who have notable proven wisdom and guidance to impart if you keep your spirit and mind open to receive instruction. Proverbs 1:5 says, *"A wise man will hear, and will increase learning; and a man of understanding shall attain unto wise counsels."*

One of the best and most challenging tasks I have ever done was climbing the Dunn's River Falls in Ocho Rios, Jamaica. We were celebrating our thirtieth wedding anniversary, and we wanted to experience all the magnificent beauty and wonder of Jamaica. The Dunn's River Falls is a never-ending flow and rapid fall, as well as a swift cascading of waterfalls that dispense directly into the Caribbean Sea. A true Jamaican treasure. The day started off wonderfully with extreme sunshine and a group of young couples who were eager to experience the thrill of nature. I remember thinking, *We are the middle-aged couple in this group, so we will have to work hard to keep up.* We boarded the charter van full of excitement! Upon our arrival I noticed other groups of climbers ready to start their climb. The instructor eagerly gathered our group together and then began explaining what was getting ready to happen.

I thought immediately his tone sounded a little too seriously pointed. I instantly felt a surge of anxiety rush through my body. *Red alert, red alert, what have you signed up for?* The instructions went something like this: "You have signed up for the adventure of a lifetime. This adventure is extremely rigorous and dangerous. We must all stick together to make it through this. Please put away all objects and clothes that can be swept away because we will be encountering swift-moving water. The water is very strong and can sweep away clothes, eyewear, hats, and all items not securely attached. Does anyone need to make adjustments?"

The tour guide assured us he was well qualified to take us on this climb. He proceeded to tell us how long he had been working at the site and that the six-hundred-foot climb would be fun and exhilarating and not to worry, if we stuck together, we would become instant friends. A waterfall! On our thirtieth anniversary we decided to climb a six-hundred-foot waterfall. *How did I get myself into this?* Our guide must have noticed the uncertainty in my eyes because he instinctively began to call me "queen." "No worries, my queen sister, your husband will guard his queen with his life." Somehow those words brought immediate affirmation to our quest, and off we went.

The strategy for this climb was for all the climbers to climb together. We were strategically positioned male, female, and male. *Okay, I'm calm. I have my water shoes on, and I'm positioned between two men. I think this can work.* I immediately introduced myself to my partner, who would be leading me, and to my pleasant surprise, his name was Dwayne.

"Dwayne, my son-in-law is named Dwayne," I said, "so you got me, right?"

He said, "Yes, just hold my hand as tight as you need, and we will get to the top and back down with no injuries."

Together Dwayne, Shaun, and I along with the rest of our team spent a couple of hours climbing slippery rocks, cascading waterfalls, and hidden caves. We had a few slips, heavy pulls, and slow and careful foot placements, but the group of twenty-five couples with a wide variety of ages, ailments, and handicaps made it up and down the waterfall without one single injury. Dwayne was instantly my friend! I didn't have to think about it. I knew we needed each other to reach our summit. I had to trust a stranger with my safety, and the result was a triumphant accomplishment. Trusting what works even when it's unfamiliar to you can reveal unyielding surplus.

As you're adjusting your decisions to now accommodate the reality of your newfound wisdom, you open your heart to receive all the good things that produce and nurture life. The hardest work isn't necessarily the actual climb, but in my opinion, it's the preparation and the moment you stand at the base of the mountain.

Proverbs 13:18 says, *"If you ignore criticism, you will end in poverty and disgrace; if you accept correction, you will be honored."*

All the hard stuff is done way before the climb, during the team work that makes the dream work. Who is on your team? Do you listen to their criticisms, instructions, and proven wisdom? The skilled and battle-tested team God has given you has wisdom, talent, and anointing to help you reach your summit. There are also times when you may need to call in a specialist, someone who has a specific skill set to help you resolve and conquer so you receive the maximum return for your labor. *"It is pleasant, to see dreams come true, but fools refuse to turn from evil to attain them";* that's what Proverbs 13:19 says.

When your quality of air has improved, your oxygen improves, and as a result of better air quality, your brain fog dissipates and a world of possibilities comes into view and focus. The second I had fulfilled the dream of My Monday becoming a mountain that I could finally learn the skill set to climb, conquer, and stand at the summit and proclaim, *"Not only did I climb you, I have now made you my launching pad to higher heights!"* I was well on my way to keep improving my skills and trying harder mountain climbs.

> *"But those who trust in the Lord will find new strength. They will soar high on wings like eagles"* (Isaiah 40:31, NLT).

Notes

How is your mountain view?

_____

_____

_____

_____

_____

_____

_____

_____

_____

_____

_____

_____

_____

_____

_____

_____

_____

_____

_____

_____

_____

About the Author

Teresa M. Cooper is cofounder/ co-pastor of New Creation Family Church, located in Shreveport, Louisiana. She received the Lord into her life at an early age. Teresa's love for the hurting and marginalized propelled her into a life of service that has now spanned twenty-five-plus years. In addition to presiding as co-pastor / executive administrator of New Creation Family Church, she is also the executive director of Family Resources for Education and Empowerment Inc., a nonprofit organization impacting and transforming the lives of at-risk youth within the public-school system. Teresa's national and global reach is seen in her service as Co-leader of Legacy Leadership Alliance, bridging the gap within denominations and cultures. Teresa actively travels throughout the country imparting the Word of God in a candid and refreshing way. She is a successful business owner, licensed nail technician, BMI songwriter, and praise and worship leader. In 2008 she added author to her title with the release of her first book, *Conquering Your Day*. 2018 she became an influencer as the creator and host of SisterFriends Cups and Conversations. The wife of Bishop Shaun D. Cooper and the mother of two—Shaun Jr. (married to Monique Brown-Cooper) and Crystal Cooper-Taylor (married to Dwayne Taylor Jr.). After thirty-three years of marriage, Teresa gleefully joined the grandma club with the births of her three grandsons—Dwayne Jr., Shaun III, and Israel Cooper—and two granddaughters, Lillian Marie and Naomi Nicole.

CPSIA information can be obtained
at www.ICGtesting.com
Printed in the USA
LVHW040030270720
661579LV00004B/530

9 781098 031800